# HOW TO RISE FROM

## THE ASHES OF TRAGEDY

by

PAUL AND JO NAUGHTON

Grosvenor House
Publishing Limited

This book is published by
Grosvenor House Publishing Ltd
Link House
140 The Broadway, Tolworth, Surrey, KT6 7HT.
www.grosvenorhousepublishing.co.uk

A CIP record for this book
is available from the British Library

ISBN 978-1-80381-709-5
eBook ISBN 978-1-80381-710-1

*This book is dedicated to our dear children,*
*Benj and Abby. You fill our home and our hearts*
*with laughter and joy. Together, you continually*
*brighten up our lives and ministry.*

# Acknowledgements

We will always be deeply grateful to those friends and family who prayed tirelessly for us during our darkest days. Without them, this book would never have been written.

To Ken and Lois Gott for bringing God's wonderful healing power into our lives through their love and ministry.

To Tim Collins for his unstinting support through many drafts of this book and for his glorious editing skills.

To Temi and Mary Ewuosho, whose practical demonstrations of love always warm our hearts.

And to our Church family for their love, support, and friendship.

# Contents

# Endorsement

I believe this book which expounds Biblical truth is a valuable tool in the hands of anyone captured in a dark and difficult season in their lives. I also believe that the principles that empowered this young couple will be of great value to anyone who reads and desires their faith to be built in God.

It was over thirty-five years ago that a young teenage girl sat in our front room seeking to be baptized in the Holy Spirit. Life, hope, and certainty for the destiny she was called to radiated from her.

So, Jo Naughton – who was then Jo Harvey – with tears streaming down her cheeks began her journey of surrender to the purposes of God for her life, wherever that would take her and whatever it would cost.

Who was to know that having moved to our capital city of London and there marry a young man, also called of God, they would plant and pastor a great church? Then together face an unimaginable tragedy, turn it to triumph, and in the process learn lessons they can share with us today.

In this wonderful book, Paul and Jo Naughton take the reader on the journey with them. Embracing the cost of the call, facing sorrow and despair yet emerging triumphant, and faith filled with great hope and purpose for the future.

Ken Gott
*Revivalist, Conference Speaker*
*from Sunderland, England*

# Chapter 1

# TRAGEDY

Many precious people are plunged into life-shattering circumstances and don't know how to cope or where to turn. Due to no fault of their own, they find themselves in dreadful circumstances. Personal calamity has many faces – betrayal, bereavement, bankruptcy, divorce, chronic sickness. The list goes on, and the effects can be devastating.

We need to be equipped by God's Word to handle tragedy just as much as we need to learn how to live in triumph. Sometimes we may want to hide from pain or pretend that disaster does not exist. But devastating things can happen to good people. To deny this can be very costly to our faith. Matthew 7:24-25 says, "Therefore whoever hears these sayings of Mine, and does them, I will liken him to a wise man who built his house on the rock: and the rain descended, the floods came, and the winds blew and beat on that house…" Jesus made it clear. The storms of life batter the wise just as they do the foolish.

# The Road to Recovery

We have written this book to help people recover from heartbreaking catastrophes and to discover how they can rise out of the ashes in strength. The Bible says: "In the world you WILL have tribulation, but fear not, I HAVE overcome the world." (John 16:33)

There are many stories of people who have come through great personal trials into victory. One of the most inspiring is the account of King David at Ziklag. It was at the city of Ziklag that David apparently lost everything; his family, his possessions, his home. The city became synonymous with tragedy for the great warrior, and yet he overcame. Through the Bible's account of his experience, God has given us a template for how to triumph over tragedy. And from our own personal experience, we can tell you that this template works.

This book is partly a Biblical study, it is partly our testimony, but it is also an instruction manual to enable you to exit tragedy. Your Ziklag experience can be just down the road. Maybe only a telephone call away. You don't usually arrive at Ziklag; Ziklag arrives at you. It has a particular knock, a particular sound, and a particular feeling in the pit of your stomach.

No reason is good enough to explain the pain that countless precious souls suffer. The sheer pointlessness of many tragedies can leave people bewildered, confused, and utterly broken-hearted. Please know right at the outset that there is a way out. If you are in the middle of a terrible catastrophe right now, know that our love and prayers are with you. As you read, by God's grace, you will find your way out of your own Ziklag.

# The Scars of Suffering

Life's journey takes us through many twists and turns and, without David's example of how to overcome catastrophe, we can find ourselves in a never-ending cycle of bitterness and remorse. Many good people carry the painful scars of difficult experiences to the grave.

Professionals will often tell a grieving soul that they will never get over the trauma of loss. As a result, many believe that there is no way out, that they will be suffering with this pain for the rest of their days. However, God says something different. Psalms 147:3 (AMP) states, "He heals the brokenhearted and binds up their wounds [curing their pains and their sorrows]."

People with similar tragic experiences to yours who have never recovered will sometimes draw near and surround you with their own pain. Although they mean to help, the wreckage of their lives may unwittingly try to suffocate you in the midst of your own suffering. We need to know what Scripture says, then make a decision to believe it and act on His Word rather than on people's opinions.

Well-meaning onlookers may tell you that failure, disaster, and pain are God's will for your life. That somehow you were chosen for calamity because you are special. That this is your cross to bear. If you don't know what the Lord has to say, you may end up trapped by sadness for a very long time. Unfortunately, time does not heal, it just buries pain.

# Your Divine Design

Everybody at one time or another experiences tragedy. Some folks recover remarkably quickly. Others become confused and weighed down, wondering how they can ever find a way out. Many live their entire lives under the shadow of disappointment and regret. We were not designed to live under the ashes of a Ziklag experience. Even the way human tissue repairs itself after cuts and bruises shows that you and I were designed to be restored. God has made the way for you to be healed and made whole, even after terrible suffering. Isaiah 53:5b (AMP) says, "...with the stripes [that wounded] Him we are healed and made whole."

We believe that this book will help anyone who has suffered a tragedy, as well as those wanting to help loved ones in times of trouble. It will equip you to confront pain with a Scriptural understanding. Jesus Himself said that He came so that we can live "life more abundantly" (John 10:10). There is no evidence that tragedy changes this Word. There *is* recovery, restoration, and healing available, even after the most difficult disasters. There is life after tragedy. Let's pray.

**Heavenly Father,**

I come to You with an open heart. I don't want to live with any hidden hurts. I don't want to get buried under the ashes of tragedy. So, I choose today to take You at

Your Word and embark on a journey to restoration. I ask You to shine Your light into the depths of my heart. Please reveal, and then heal, my buried pain.

Have Your way in my heart and life, I pray.

In Jesus' name,

Amen.

# Chapter 2

# DAVID'S DARKEST DAYS

Let's go back three thousand years in history to the place where David faced tragedy and devastation. Ziklag was a well-fortified city in ancient Israel. Our young warrior David lived there with his family, using the location as a military base from which to go out to battle. Located in the Negev desert, it was relatively safe from raiders. It had changed hands a couple of times between the Israelites and the Philistines. At this point in history, David was liked by both camps. Ziklag was only about eighteen miles from the major garrison city of Gaza, so there was not much need for military security. David and his loyal band of followers therefore felt quite safe there. It is often when we feel most safe that the effects of tragedy can hit hardest. When unexpected disaster hits, the shock and pain can be great.

In the Scriptures, our hero David returns after a three-day journey from an abortive battle. Smoke is rising in the distance, and the unthinkable has happened. The closer they get to their home, the more evident it becomes that everything has been totally destroyed. The writer states: "Then it happened when David and his men came to Ziklag on the third day, that the Amalekites had made a raid on the Negev and on Ziklag, and had overthrown Ziklag and burned it with fire; and they took captive the women and all who were in it, both small and great, without killing anyone, and carried them off and went their way. And when David and his men came to the city, behold it was burned with fire, and their wives and their sons and their daughters had been taken captive. Then David and the people who were with him lifted up their voices and wept until there was no strength in them to weep." (1 Samuel 30:1-4)

# The Truth About Tragedy

Modern tragedies may include a marriage which suddenly breaks down, a promising business venture that goes bust, the death of a loved one, a shock redundancy after years of dedicated service, a freak car accident, or a completely unexpected medical complication. These experiences usually contain strange ingredients which don't add up. They lead us to think: 'If only he hadn't gone to that party'; 'If only she had caught an earlier plane'; 'Why didn't our midwife see that there was something wrong?' Why him? Why her? Why me?

Let's go back to one of Jesus' parables. Jesus told us that the storms of life will come to everyone. To believers and non-believers. To men and women of faith, and to doubters. To those who hear and do what Jesus says, as well as to those who hear but don't do what He says. The rains fell (pressure on both types of house from above), the winds blew (pressure on both types of house from the sides), and the floods came (pressure on both types of house from beneath). The inevitability of storms is probably not the most popular thing Jesus taught, but it is nevertheless true.

If the enemy can make you believe that you should be exempt from suffering, it will add untold misery to times of adversity. Sadly, because we live in a fallen world, suffering is inevitable. Let's read the words of Jesus again. Matthew 7:24-27 reads, "Therefore, everyone who hears these words of mine and acts on them may be compared to a wise man who built his house on the rock. And the rain fell, and the floods came, and the winds blew and slammed against that house; and yet it did not fall, for it had been founded on the rock. Everyone who hears these words of mine and does not act on them will be like a foolish man who built his house on the sand. The rains fell, and the floods came, and the winds blew and slammed against that house; and it fell – and great was its fall."

A rich man often declares that his wealth is a strong defense against such storms (Proverbs 10:15). A 'faith' man will declare diplomatic immunity from adversity. Of course, there are certain storms that we must rebuke as Jesus did, but everyone will at some stage encounter tragedy.

# Facing Every Season

Our job is not to debate whether storms will or won't come, but to live in Christ and be equipped for every situation. We have many examples in the Bible of mighty men and women who suffered tragedy. Abraham lost his beloved nephew, Lot; Jacob believed his son of destiny, Joseph, was dead; Job lost his children and his livelihood; Naomi lost her husband and her sons; Mary watched her miracle child die; Peter failed his greatest test and then lost his friend, James; Paul was shipwrecked, betrayed, and abandoned. The list goes on.

We often minister to people who have faced life-shattering experiences. There was a man who had been raped at the tender age of twelve. The experience and the power of those memories emotionally crippled him for decades. There was a woman who committed her life to the scrapheap after her first husband divorced her and her second husband died. The family who suddenly lost two children. The woman whose father died too young. But all these individuals rose out of pain and devastation to receive healing and true restoration.

Dreams can be shattered in many different ways. For David, his dreams literally went up in smoke. Even from a distance, he could see that his home and his city were gone.

When the bubble of the perfect (or even imperfect) life bursts, the pain is often impossible to bear. In the days and weeks after a calamity, what is inside your heart will come out of your mouth. We know what we are talking about, we have passports with 'Tragedy' stamped on several pages! Everyone is affected by devastation at some point, but only some come out the other side stronger. How to arise from tragedy is the real issue, not whether or not you'll be hit.

You may be in the middle of a calamity right now. You're in the right place, keep reading. Alternatively, all may be well. If that's you, please read with just as much attention. You can equip yourself now so that when adversity comes, you know the way out. It is always better to be prepared. Let's pray.

**Heavenly Father,**

I don't want to get stuck in tragedy. I don't want to be defined by adversity, so I ask You to show me how to deal with life's storms. Just as David came out the other side of calamity, I ask that You would help me to find my way out of every difficulty. I recognize that suffering is inevitable. I know that over the course of my life, I will face fiery trials, so I ask You to lead me out every time so that I can continually grow stronger.

In Jesus' name I pray,

Amen.

# Chapter 3

# OUR STORY OF LOSS

Naomi was our first daughter, and our only child at the time. She was a healthy, blonde-haired girl, with blue eyes and a magnetic personality. We were pastoring a small but growing church in London, England. We were known in Christian circles as a promising young ministry with a bright future. The eyes of the church and our world were upon us, tracking our progress and encouraging us on to greater things.

On the morning of Tuesday, 4th April, 2000, we took Naomi to the doctor. She had been up all night with a temperature which normal medication could not reduce. Just nineteen months old, Naomi was limp and lethargic. The clinician called an ambulance and we arrived at our local hospital at noon.

The doctor in charge put her under observation and we waited for further progress. We waited and waited, seeking help, but none came. We begged for her to be given medicine, but the doctor delayed, wishing to wait for a urine sample. When Naomi had her first seizure at around ten-thirty that evening it was obvious that something was very, very wrong. More and more doctors arrived at her bedside throughout that long night until there was a team of about fifteen from different hospitals working to save her life.

# Declared Dead

Our sweetheart suffered three cardiac arrests and catastrophic organ failure. She was declared dead at eight o'clock the following morning. The killer – bacterial meningitis – could have been stopped in its tracks by a precautionary dose of antibiotics on arrival at the accident and emergency department – standard practice in these circumstances at most hospitals.

As the doctors disconnected the life support machines and pulled out their drug lines from her lifeless frame, our lives crashed. We wrapped her body in a sheet and left the room. We were flooded with unimaginable pain. She was our love, our treasure, our angel. And now she was gone.

Until our terrible loss, we had assumed that tragedy was a trial experienced by people who had no faith. From the moment of our salvation, we had been taught to walk by faith, to speak God's Word, to never make a negative confession.

We watched over our words like hawks. We can honestly say that we never spoke a single negative word over our little daughter. Yet here we were, driving back from the hospital without our darling, wondering what on earth to do next.

# God Is Able

We believed in the resurrection of the dead and had heard recent stories of such miracles taking place, so we gathered a small army of prayer warriors and went back to the hospital on the afternoon of the day Naomi died. We prayed there for two hours and then set up rotational teams to keep interceding until something happened. She died on a Wednesday morning, and we prayed until the Saturday afternoon.

One of the saddest things I (Paul) ever had to do was to remove her baby seat from our car and place it in her now empty bedroom.

Naomi was the church's baby, too. Everybody loved her. Her funeral drew nearly five hundred mourners, people so broken by the news that all they could do was cry. It felt like even the flowers were crying.

We deliberately chose a bigger coffin than necessary to try and lessen the sadness, and we requested that all mourners should wear bright colors. But our efforts failed. Sorrow prevailed.

# The Power of Pain

There is no tranquilizer to kill such pain. It sits in your soul, eats and drinks with you, sleeps with you, and wakes up with you every morning. It looks at you in the mirror and holds you in its cold, cruel arms.

As the pastor of our church, I (Paul) felt so guilty that everyone I had so vigorously encouraged to join our walk of faith was a victim with us, trapped in this pain. The eyes of the church were now on us for a different reason. People who had once laughed and joked with us now found it hard to fellowship with us. Many didn't know what to say and didn't know whether to mention the elephant in the room. I (Paul) felt like I had led the whole church into absolute defeat and the feeling was killing me. How could we ever recover?

If you are in the middle of a terrible calamity, we want you to know that there is a way out of devastation. Psalm 23 is not just a beautiful excerpt often read at funerals. It is God's Word, and it is filled with promise. Psalms 23:4 (TPT) says, "Lord, even when your path takes me through the valley of deepest darkness, fear will never conquer me, for you already have. You remain close to me and lead me through it all the way. Your authority is my strength and my peace. The comfort of your love takes away my fear. I'll never be lonely, for you are near." We came out of the other side of our calamity, and you can, too. Let's pray.

**Heavenly Father,**

There is so much pain in the world, and it feels like I have gone through more than my fair share of suffering. I ask You to help me to face every sadness that has sunk to the bottom of my soul. I don't want to run away from my pain because that won't make it go away. Instead, I choose to look at the griefs and sorrows of my life and to bring them all to You.

Thank You that You are right beside me, even when I walk through The Valley of the Shadow of Death.

I open my heart to You, Oh Lord.

In Jesus' name, I pray.

Amen.

# Chapter 4

# A TIME TO CRY

The psalmist wrote: "Weeping may endure for the night, but joy comes in the morning." (Psalm 30:5) The trouble is, we may not know how far away 'morning' is. Some people's experiences are so tragic that they may feel like there will never be a sunrise again. That could be the way you are feeling right now. One thing is certain, though: morning will come. But mourning must come first.

After Naomi died, we wept. But we grieved differently. Paul needed solitude in order to grieve, so I (Jo) made plans to give him time alone. I cried in Paul's arms and in the company of my closest friends. I wept in secret corners of corridors at work, and behind the pages of a book on public transport. I made a promise to myself that I would never push my pain down. I instinctively understood that it was better out than trapped inside. We mourned differently, but we both wept – a great deal.

# The Power of Weeping

In our original story, David the great warrior weeps. He weeps and weeps. Very often, people jump to the part in David's story when he encouraged himself in the Lord. But that was not what he did first. 1 Samuel 30:4 says, "Then David and the people who were with him lifted up their voices and wept, until they had no more power to weep." David and his mighty warriors wept, and they wept hard. They did not hold back; they let their pain out. Crying in these circumstances is not a sign of weakness; it leads to strength. If you have not yet cried freely, we are praying that God will give you an anointing to weep. It is the first step on the road to recovery, and it is where healing begins.

One of the world's major religions teaches its followers to rid themselves of feelings in order to reach spiritual heights. In certain cultures, crying is frowned upon and seen as a sign of frailty or immaturity. Even in normal families, parents often tell young children not to cry when they are hurt or sad. Many people become afraid of their own emotions – afraid of losing control or breaking down.

This is in complete contrast to God's Word, which says: "…Pour out your heart like water before the face of the Lord…" (Lamentations 2:19b). In the Bible, many strong men of God shed tears. Joseph wept bitterly and loudly on many occasions; Jeremiah poured his heart out before God and was known as the weeping prophet; Jesus wept when He saw Mary and Martha's pain; and Paul wept when he left his Ephesian brothers for the last

17

time. Aside from his Ziklag experience, David soaked his bed from crying all night long. Psalms 6:6 says, "I am weary with my groaning; All night I make my bed swim; I drench my couch with my tears."

# Releasing Pain

After years of suppression, many dear people have to be liberated so that they can cry again. According to the Scriptures, man is made up of three parts: spirit, soul, and body. The reborn human spirit produces living water (see John 7:38). The human body emits water in the form of urine, but the healthy human soul should also be able to produce water in the form of tears. Weeping is the heart's way of releasing emotional toxins produced by stress and strain. Crying is both healing and liberating.

If you have never been able to express grief, disappointment, or sadness through tears, and Jesus is already your Lord, ask the Holy Spirit to show you why. Ask Him right now to flood your heart with His healing power and to unblock your soul. If Jesus isn't yet your King, invite Him to come into your life immediately and to help you on the journey to a marvelous restoration.

Jesus is *the* Master Restorer. He bought and paid for your total healing and restoration when He hung on the cross. Isaiah 53:3 calls Him, "A Man of sorrows and acquainted with grief." There is no pain or heartache that He does not understand. He knows how you feel right now, and He is ready to restore your precious soul.

Isaiah 53:4 explains, "Surely He has borne our griefs and carried our sorrows..." Jesus carried every one of your hurts when He hung upon the cross. He is the Master Healer, and releasing your pain before Him is the first step towards your recovery. Let's pray.

**Heavenly Father,**

I have so much sadness inside. The things that I have suffered have weighed me down and caused me too much sorrow. But I don't want to carry this pain any longer.

(*Now tell the Lord what you have gone through, in as much detail as possible. Be honest about any confusion or questions that you have. Share your thoughts and feelings with Him.*)

As I pour out my heart before You, Lord, I ask You to fill me afresh with Your wonderful love. Where I feel raw inside, I thank You for releasing Your healing balm into my heart and soul.

I receive Your perfect peace, and I surrender to Your love.

In Jesus' name I pray,

Amen.

# Chapter 5

# THE PRAISE LEVER

Praising God in these circumstances never makes sense to the natural mind. It seems pointless and misplaced. It goes against every emotion. People fear for your sanity. However, the very same David who sat among the ashes of his ruined city strengthened himself in the Lord, through praise and encouragement:

"Now David was greatly distressed... But David strengthened himself in the Lord his God." (1 Samuel 30:6) Later, the very same David wrote this in Psalm 8:2: "Out of the mouths of babes and infants you have ordained praise, because of your adversaries, to make your enemies and the avenger cease."

In the midst of tragedy and suffering, we can often hear the scornful, mocking voices of our enemy, the devil, louder than ever. Praise will shut his mouth and bring confusion to his camp (see 2 Chronicles 20:17-22). Even when the enemy we are facing is death itself, praise will silence his taunts and confound his destructive plans. And more importantly, praise brings God near.

In the days and weeks after Naomi died, both of us found a way through the wall of pain that was pressing in on every side. We broke through the barrier differently, but we both came out the other side. These are our stories.

# Jo's Offering

Bewilderment followed me everywhere I went in the days and weeks after Naomi died. Reading the Word was a struggle: I saw healing on almost every page, which at times stirred confusion. Prayer just led to tears of pain and frustration. It sounds bizarre, but rejoicing became my refuge. When I praised Jesus, I forgot my grief, even if just for a moment. Praise brought me relief. One song became my 'go to', and I believe the words inadvertently paved the way to my restoration. I would spin around as I sang: "You have turned my mourning into dancing. You have turned my sorrow into joy." Praise became a prophecy that was eventually fulfilled, despite my inability at the time to imagine life without grief.

# Paul's Sacrifice of Praise

At our daughter's funeral, I lifted my hands to the Lord as I sang, and I even found the strength to comfort others. In the days that followed, I fought off physical sickness, panic attacks, and insomnia, but I couldn't kill the pain. It was like a heavy rock. About a week after Naomi's funeral, I sat on the floor of her bedroom, opposite her cot, and wept. Right then I said to God:

"Lord, I have no song left in my heart. Please accept this act as a sacrifice of praise." I wound up her little toy mobile which hung above her crib and played a tune. I sat there in a pool of tears as the notes echoed around the empty room. This was my sacrifice of praise. It was all I could manage to do, but I believe it was enough.

To move a heavy rock, you first need to put a lever underneath it. That lever for us was the sacrifice of praise. I believe God received our offerings and He unlocked the pain in our hearts. Our journey to recovery had begun.

Many dear people trapped in the grip of addiction are merely trying to dull the agony of past traumas. Some folk go off into the realm of fantasy, creating fictional childhoods, because the reality of their own experiences is too painful. Others just deny the hurt, but the effects of it revisit them continually. Understanding where you're at on the journey is really important, because it most certainly is a journey.

If there is any pain left inside you, let praise from your lips begin to lever the heavy stone of grief out of your heart. Ask the Holy Spirit to take you right back there now, to the point of separation or devastation, and start praising Jesus as best you know how in the midst of the pain.

There may be trapped words, emotions, or tears in your soul as a result of your experience. Start to release them into God's presence. Present Him with a sacrifice of praise on the altar of destruction. At the darkest time in our lives, God turned our agony into an altar of sacrifice. Our praises in the midst of disaster became our exit from paralyzing pain. Let's pray.

**Heavenly Father,**

Even in the place of devastation, even at the lowest point in my life, I choose to praise. Even as I stand in the ashes of tragedy, I rejoice. I declare that You are a good, good Father. I declare that You are faithful through every season. I declare that You are worthy of all my praise. I give You the glory for all the great things that You can do. And I declare: You have turned my mourning into dancing, You have turned my sorrow into joy.

I thank You for Your everlasting love.

In Jesus' name I pray,

Amen.

# Chapter 6

# BUT WHY?

Even the night she was dying, I (Paul) held our little darling's feet whilst on my knees, praying for God's mercy to visit us. She slowly slipped away.

When something goes wrong, what is the first question that most people ask God – even if they don't believe He exists? Why would God allow this? Why did this happen?

Imagine now that you are David. You're anointed by the Lord and known as a man after God's own heart. You have brought victory to an entire nation. You are a mighty man of breakthrough. You go out to fight for God in obedience to the leading of His Spirit. However, on your way back to Ziklag, when you're still some distance from home, you see that your entire city is on fire. Your belongings, and possibly your whole family, are gone. You are God's man, but you are in the midst of disaster. And yet you never ask God, 'Why?' Wow.

# Why Has God Allowed This?

When we were thrust into the midst of tragedy, the questions on everyone's lips were: 'Why has God allowed this? Why did Satan get away with such a devastating blow?' 'Why didn't God heal this sweet, innocent girl?' 'Why didn't He raise her from the dead and prove His great power to the world?'

No-one was more perturbed by these questions than me (Jo). At the time, I had just finished working for Prince (now King) Charles. I was the VP for Communications for his world-famous charity, The Prince's Trust. I had met many times with him, his top staff, the UK's Prime Minister, and various government, industry, and entertainment bigwigs. Imagine the splash that an infant resurrection could make. I worked with journalists from the biggest newspapers in the land. Wow, the opportunity! But still our daughter's short life was over.

We searched the whole Bible for answers and inevitably ended up reading the book of Job. If you removed all the whys and various attempts at explanation from Job, you wouldn't be left with much. Job's story was one of tremendous suffering and loss. Worry opened the door to terrible devastation. The trauma he endured at the hands of the devil was more than anyone could have imagined.

We found all manner of reasons why people in the Bible suffered death and injury. God told Elijah that King Ahab's children would suffer early death due to Ahab's sin (1 Kings 21:29). David lost the baby son born to him out of wedlock. The children of Israel in Jeremiah's time suffered death because of the judgment of God on the people. Elijah proclaimed a three-and-a-half-year famine which killed many (1 Kings 17:1), and so on. But the Bible's tragedies did not help us to understand why our daughter had died.

I wrestled with the question of why for three or four months, asking God to show me what had happened, what had gone wrong. I thought that if I understood the tragedy, I could begin my healing journey. As I sought God's face, He answered.

# No Answer Is Enough

I sensed the Lord ask me if I could imagine a good enough reason why our little girl had to die. Of course I could not! The Lord showed me that even if He gave me an explanation, it would never be good enough to justify the loss of our little girl. No reason would ever be sufficient to explain the death of our dear daughter. How could it be?

The Lord then took me deeper. God showed me that in ancient Hebrew (the language of the Old Testament), terms such as 'why' and 'how' come from a root word which means chaos. I realized that continuing to ask why would hold me in a state of confusion, chaos, and turbulence. While I focused my energy on finding answers, I realized that I would only stay trapped in a world of grief and disappointment.

I made a monumental decision. I chose to lay down *why* as a sacrificial offering before the Lord. Coming before God, the silent tears dripping from my eyes, I laid down my right to an answer. I gave the Lord every one of my questions as an offering. Ceasing to ask why became an act of surrender for both of us. And it turned out to be one of the best decisions that we ever made in the midst of that turmoil.

On many occasions, having faith and asking why are activities which are enemies of each other. If God's agenda for our lives is restoration, then sitting around in the muck and the ashes of a ruined life and asking why will only delay our escape from the pain.

We came to realize that, from God's point of view, the most important question for us wasn't why but "how do we get out of this place of devastation?" And "how do we get back to a place of victory where we belong?"

Asking why just took us in the wrong direction. It made our hurt and grief all the more bewildering. Instead, we learned to say: "Lord, I don't know why all this happened. But I want to know how to get out of this pain and how to get healed and restored."

This led us towards palpable relief. Being preoccupied with 'Why?' can be a very heavy weight. Laying it down leads to lightness and liberty. We opened the doors of our hearts to His healing love and, without realizing it, a new ministry of bringing healing and restoration to others was born.

# Laying Down Why

If you have been bewildered by why, unable to understand how tragedy or catastrophe was able to knock at your door or the door of someone you love, we would like to encourage you to do what we did. Come to the Lord in prayer and bring all your questions to Him as a sacrificial offering. Lay why down at the Cross and ask Jesus to start to bring His healing into your life in exchange.

When you are sufficiently far from the pain, when you are well on the road to recovery, it may be safe to ask a few questions about your ordeal. Once you have received His healing, you may find that it is helpful. But for now, we suggest you take the brave step of laying your questions down. Let's pray.

**Heavenly Father,**

I don't understand why I have suffered so much. I don't know why the people I love have endured such pain. It does not seem fair, and the sense of injustice is agony.

But I now realize that holding onto my questions will keep me bound to torment. So, I make a monumental decision today. I give up every question that has caused me so much confusion. I lay down why as a sacrificial offering at the foot of the Cross. I give it all to You, Lord Jesus. I give up my right to an answer. I surrender my all to You, Lord.

Now I ask You to reach into the depths of my heart and take my pain away. I surrender the sadness that was trapped under my confusion. I pour out my pain like water before Your face.

In exchange for my questions and confusion, I ask You to fill my heart with Your precious healing love. I receive Your peace into the depths of my soul.

Thank You, Lord, that I have begun my journey to freedom.

In Jesus' name I pray,

Amen.

# Chapter 7

# TRUE RESTORATION

There is a huge difference between pretending to be strong and being strong. In the same way, there is a great gulf between trying to appear healed and being healed. We must never pretend anything. We must always know ourselves well enough to know if and where we hurt. Buried pain can often cause problems in unexpected areas of our lives. It can even lead to sickness. Study after study has revealed a connection between unresolved emotional pain and diseases such as arthritis, cancer, and dementia.

## The Caverns of Your Soul

Proverbs 20:27 says: "The spirit of man is the candle of the Lord, searching out the inner caverns of the soul." The human soul has many caverns – secret caves or rooms containing pictures, sounds, smells, emotions, and other details of life's experiences. Have you ever heard a song and instantly been transported back to a particular place? Has a specific taste or fragrance ever caused a forgotten recollection to flood your consciousness? Memories are parceled up in our souls, ready to be opened at any time. In a flash, a face or name can bring you back to an event that took place decades ago.

I (Jo) remember a day when I walked into our daughter's room several weeks after her death. I decided it was time to sort out all her clothes and shoes. As I opened her closet door, I was overwhelmed by an unexpected waft of Naomi's sweet fragrance. Instantly my daughter was back in my arms. I broke down and wept, pouring out my pain once more. As the sadness lifted, the Lord's healing love filled my heart.

If you ask God, He will use your daily life to reveal hidden memories and open the closed caverns of your soul. When that happens, please call out to Him for His healing. Lamentations 2:19b says, "...Pour out your heart like water before the presence of the Lord..." Tell Him what hurts and why it hurts; ask Him to take away your pain. He is your Healer, and He is able to restore your heart, one precious piece at a time.

# The Importance of Your Healing

It is important to understand that the healing of your soul is *just as important* to God as healing your physical body. Let's look at Isaiah 61:1-2: "The Spirit of the Lord God is upon me, Because the Lord has anointed me to bring good news to the afflicted; He has sent me to bind up the broken hearted, To proclaim liberty to captives, And freedom to prisoners... To comfort all who mourn."

The verses above describe the reasons Jesus came to earth. They reflect God's heart towards you and me. Affliction is both an inner and outer condition. When your heart is broken, it is of course entirely an issue of the soul. Captivity and imprisonment speak of both inner and outer struggles; comfort, of course, is a ministry to the heart. We can see from this passage the importance that the Lord places on bringing restoration to your soul.

There are healing crusades where multitudes come to receive miracles. Mighty men and women of God have ministered under the Holy Spirit's anointing in awesome displays of God's mastery over sickness and disease. We thank God for all of this, but we know through the passage in Isaiah that God is just as concerned about healing our souls. The anointing on Jesus was to heal both the inner and the outer person.

In Proverbs 18:14, it says: "A wounded spirit, who can bear?" The pain is too great for us to carry. But we don't have to carry it. The price has been paid for our inner agonies as well as our outer afflictions. As Jesus offered His body on the altar of sacrifice at Calvary, He paid for man's TOTAL redemption in spirit, soul, and body. He bore your sorrow and mine. After we lost our precious little girl, we brought our sorrow to the Lord. We cried out to Him to take away our pain and bring healing to our hearts.

The Bible boldly declares that: "Surely our griefs He himself bore, And our sorrows He carried." (Isaiah 53:4) This is proof enough that we should stand against griefs and sorrows in the same way that we should stand against sin and sickness. We need to acknowledge our pain and call out to God for our healing until we are completely restored. You will know when you are fully restored because it won't hurt anymore.

Any doctor will tell you that there is a definite link between inner and outer wellbeing. Sometimes sickness and premature death are linked to unhealed inner griefs and sorrows. The healing of the heart can lead to the healing of the body.

Many people carry the pain of a bitter and painful divorce, bringing wreckage straight into another marriage. We need to invite the Holy Spirit into those caverns of the soul which are filled with the root causes of separation, rejection, sorrow, or grief.

# Facing Your Pain

Just as we did, ask God to bring you back to painful memories and pour out your heart to Him about what you went through, detail by detail. Psalm 62:8 tells us to: "Trust in Him at all times, oh people, and pour out your heart."

Jesus is a Master Restorer, and He has personally paid for your restoration. He has wonderful ways of helping us to face our pain in order that we can be healed. There have been many testimonies of people who were brought back to a traumatic event in life by re-encountering similar circumstances. For example, returning to a certain hospital or seeing tell-tale signs of betrayal in a new marriage.

In the Gospel of John, we see a vivid example of how Jesus set the scene for the healing of one of His closest disciples. Peter, who had denied the Lord three times through the smoke and haze of a fire (see John 18:25), was then gloriously reunited with him through the smoke and haze of a fire specially prepared by Jesus Himself (see John 21:9-17). It was almost as if Jesus was deliberately taking Peter back to the setting of his denial in order to bring full restoration in his heart.

Romans 9:26 refers to this principle: "And it shall be that in the place where it was said to them, 'You are not My people,' There they shall be called sons of the living God." Maybe you need an experience like this. Maybe you need to ask Jesus to bring you back to the location of your tragedy. It's the place where you will have to face pain, but it's also the place where you can receive your healing. Trust Him to do the miracle.

Six months after our daughter died, I (Paul) was back in the same hospital praying for a child with almost identical symptoms. Fortunately, this little one pulled through, but all the memories that I relived by re-entering that hospital ward, I poured out to the Lord.

## Seeking Restoration

God describes His masterful healing another way: "For your shame you shall receive double honour." (Isaiah 61:7) What the enemy intended for your destruction, God can turn into a great testimony if you give it wholeheartedly to Him and allow Him free access to the sadness and pain.

Several weeks after our own tragedy, we began to understand that Jesus had created a remedy for life-shattering situations. Our hearts were lifted up. We heard how some friends who had suffered the death of their newborn child had received genuine healing of their pain and grief. We became desperate for such an experience. We needed this kind of medicine – and fast. So, we began to believe God for our own healing.

We were assured by God's Word that the agony of tragedy could become the birthplace of restoration. God is *such* a master at restoration that when He has finished His work on you, nobody will ever know that you were once the victim of catastrophe.

In the book of Daniel, the three Hebrew children came out of their fiery ordeal without even smelling of smoke (see Daniel 3:27). So can we. We can set our faith towards a healing which is so complete that there are no signs of former desolation. We can believe God for a grief and sorrow-free life. If Jesus has already borne our griefs and sorrows, why should we hold onto them? For us not to seek God's healing for our souls is to short-change Jesus' great sacrifice.

# Letting Go of Pain

Sometimes (especially in bereavement or separation) we may *want* to hold onto the pain, as it is often the closest reminder of the person we have lost. We can't have the person, so we'll keep the pain of their absence instead. We wish time could stop. But we must learn to release our loved ones and the pain of their absence to God in exchange for His plan of restoration.

Be assured, the wonderful gifts of kindness, fun, or friendship that loved ones have sown into our lives will live on in us. We become part of their legacy. The person has gone, but they have left behind the evidence of their love, wisdom, strength, and generosity in our lives. Holding onto the pain only keeps us in darkness. It's not easy to do, but we must release our pain and our loved ones into God's hands. We are not designed in Christ to live in the past, but to look forward to what God has in store for us: "For we are His workmanship, created in Christ Jesus for good works which He has prepared for us to walk in." (Ephesians 2:10)

There are good works that God will use you to accomplish in the lives of others. But that will happen once you have started the process of receiving your healing. Ask God to begin that work in you today. Maybe it has already begun. Ask Him to continue to heal your heart, to bring you to complete restoration. Your story will become a source of hope to others. Let's pray.

**Heavenly Father,**

I don't want to carry this pain around with me anymore. I now realize that You want to restore my soul and that You have already paid the price for the healing of my heart. I am ready to share my heartbreak with You, Lord.

(*Now tell the Lord which memories have come to mind. Tell Him what is hurting you the most and why. Tell your Heavenly Father exactly how you feel. Pour out your pain like water in His presence. If you have lost someone you love, tell the Lord that you miss them and what you miss most. Share in as much detail as possible.*)

Lord, I ask You to reach into the deep places of my heart and take my pain away. I choose to surrender my sadness, I give You all my hurts. Instead, I receive Your wonderful healing balm into the depths of my heart. Fill me up with Your love.

In Jesus' name I pray,

Amen.

# Chapter 8

# HOW OTHERS REACT

Hostility is bad at the best of times. To be facing the wrath of a crowd when your whole world has collapsed is another story. When you bear the responsibility of leadership or if you are in the public spotlight, tragedy produces extra pain. Nothing is private. The world looks on as you process the trauma, read the messages of regret, receive spiteful criticism, and mourn your loss.

1 Samuel 30: 4-6 describes what David went through: "Then David and the people that were with him lifted up their voices and wept, until they had no more power to weep... And David was greatly distressed; for the people spoke of stoning him, because the soul of all the people was grieved for all the people were embittered, each one because of his sons and daughters."

We had the blessing of being surrounded by a loving church who supported us in an extraordinary way. Yet still there was awkwardness in some of our relationships. A number of people felt personal responsibility for

Naomi's death. You could see the regret in their faces and their unspoken questions. "Why did I not take this spiritual attack on my pastors more seriously?" "Why did I not come to the hospital to pray?" "Why could I not hear God telling me to intercede?" "Why did I not see this coming?"

# Dealing With Insensitivity

It was clear that certain church leaders thought we must have been involved in some heinous crime or hidden sin to suffer such a thing. Unless someone has been through a similar tragedy or worse, it is difficult for them to relate to what you are going through. We had to be gracious at times. One pastor tried to console me (Paul) by telling me that a lot of ministries he knew were under pressure at that time, and Naomi's death probably saved us from greater tragedy further down the road. "You never know," he said. "She could have been raped and murdered as a teenager!" I remained silent as the minister vented.

The book of Job is full of the weird and strange accusations of Job's 'friends'. Like Job, we endeavored to be gracious, and to listen to and pray for our well-meaning 'friends'. Relationships are the most precious things which God has given to us, and sometimes we just need to bear with people in their awkwardness.

If people have said the wrong things to you during your time of heartbreak, it will help if you try your best to let them off. Most people don't set out to make your pain worse, they are usually trying their best, but they are on foreign ground. Another well-wisher sent us a message quoting Matthew 9:24: "She is not dead but sleeping." Those words were hard to swallow. Jesus raised that little girl from the dead, but our daughter was already buried. Again, we blessed the sender.

Another common comment people make during times of trauma or tragedy is, "Be strong!" Sometimes that can be a way of asking you not to cry. But bottling your pain is not strength; it only leads to emotional problems. Suggestions that you should be strong can seem insensitive when you're in the midst of pain. The best way to obtain strength is to throw yourself onto God. Ask Him to undergird you and help you. Ask the Lord to enable you to come out the other side strong.

# What Should I Say?

What should we say to someone suffering a devastating experience? Probably as little as possible. The people who were of most comfort to us in our time of loss were those who made the tea, washed the car, and mowed the lawn. Those who sat with us in silence. Those who listened to our shock and disbelief without offering glib answers.

The countless cards and letters people wrote were of great comfort to me (Jo). Words of compassion, sadness, and empathy helped me to face my pain. I often wept as I read the notes that came each day. The first bouquet of flowers we received meant the most. But it was the little card that helped rather than the pretty flowers. All it said was, "I'm just so very sorry." They say 'less is more', and this is seldom truer than at times of deep sadness. Let's pray.

**Heavenly Father,**

Things people have said have not always helped. Certain comments have seemed thoughtless or insensitive. But I realize that they were trying their best to offer some sort of comfort. I choose to be gracious, and I thank You for everyone who reached out during my time of need.

Thank You, Lord, that although people will get it wrong, You will always be by my number one source of comfort and support. Help me to come out of my healing journey with new strength. Also, I ask that You will use me to help others in their times of need. Help me to offer others the right support and the right words.

I love You, Lord.

In Jesus' name,

Amen.

# Chapter 9

# WATER QUENCHES FIRE

The Bible is full of imagery. Visions and types and shadows paint rich pictures to help us understand the Lord's heart and His ways. For instance, the Bible uses the image of fire to explain the impact of the Spirit of God in our lives.

Proverbs 20:27 describes His presence in our hearts: "The spirit of a man is the candle of the Lord." Hebrews 1:7 explains that we become like fire when God touches our lives: "He makes His Angels winds and His ministers a flame of fire." Matthew 3:11 speaks of us being engulfed in holy fire: "He will baptize with The Holy Spirit and fire." Finally, in Luke 12:49, Jesus said: "I have come to cast fire on the Earth and oh that it were already kindled!"

You may not consider yourself to be much of a flame of fire for God, but even the smallest candle can burn a house down. The California Fire Department stated that one discarded match may have caused nearly five billion dollars' worth of property damage when an entire region went up in flames in 2007.

Please pay extra attention to what we are about to explain about our adversary the devil. In the twelfth chapter of Revelation, he is seen behaving in his usual way as a bully, persecuting a pregnant woman in the wilderness. In this vision, he is portrayed as a fierce dragon and a vicious serpent.

Let's look at Revelation 12:15: "So the serpent spewed water out of his mouth like a flood after the woman, that he might cause her to be carried away by the flood." But whoever heard of a dragon that spews water? Aren't they supposed to spew fire? This one doesn't. Once again, the devil is exposed as having inadequate weaponry. One may legitimately accuse him of being a fake dragon.

# The Fire-Quencher

From this we see that the devil is trying to quench fire rather than breathe flames. Jesus came to baptize us with fire. The devil wants to put it out. Tragedy is often a fire-quencher. In the midst of devastating circumstances, your fire for God can be extinguished altogether under the sheer weight of pain. Standing in the smoldering ashes of a burnt life, it sometimes seems impossible to stay on fire for God and to be zealous about fulfilling His purposes.

When our sweetheart was so tragically torn from us, it seemed like our fire for God was completely put out. We felt drowned. It was not long before we realized that we would need to slowly but surely rekindle that flame so that we could enter a new season. But first, we had to dry out.

# Drying Out

God revealed to me (Paul) in His Word that Jesus Himself experienced the pain of loss on several occasions. He was a man of sorrows and acquainted with grief. Yet He was strong and full of wisdom, knowledge, and joy. The Lord showed me how the assassination of John the Baptist was a personal tragedy for Jesus and His ministry.

John was a mighty man of God, anointed with the spirit and power of Elijah. But he ended up being imprisoned and then beheaded for preaching against King Herod. In this one act of Jezebellic cunning, Jesus lost a cousin, a ministry associate, and the very forerunner of His coming.

The following passage shows how Jesus behaved straight after he received news of John's death. Mark 6:30-34 reads, "And He said to them, 'Come away by yourselves to a lonely place and rest a while.' For there were many people coming and going and they did not even have time to eat. And they went away in the boat to a lonely place by themselves. And the people saw them going, and many recognized them, and they ran there together on foot from all the cities and got there ahead of them. And when Jesus went ashore, He saw a great multitude, and felt compassion for them because they were like sheep without a shepherd; and He began to teach them many things."

Jesus showed us how to dry out through His words: "Come away by yourselves to a lonely place and rest a while." (Mark 6:31) There was a lonely place of prayer and praise that was waiting for us after our daughter died. Jesus met us there and began restoring us, piece by fragile piece.

We didn't care if we were a damp and soggy mess inside and out. We just allowed the sunshine of God's presence to start to evaporate each and every trace of the devil's attempt to drown us in mire. We have already talked about the power of praise, but God truly inhabits the praises of His people – especially when praise is a sacrifice which feels like it's costing you everything. Praise and prayer helped bring restoration. And we started to dry out.

# Remembering Others

The chapter in Mark goes on to say that Jesus was filled with compassion for the people. The Bible tells us that on the same day that He heard of John's death, Jesus fed the five thousand, walked on water, calmed the storm, and healed the sick.

I don't know about you, but if my cousin and closest ministry associate had just been assassinated in a cheap demonic plot, I would not be in the mood to help or minister to anybody. My only message to them would be: "I've just lost a close relative and ministry friend. Go away and don't be so selfish."

Jesus didn't even think about pushing the people away. The dragon had just spewed some icy cold water on Jesus, and yet He responded to those who needed Him with selfless love and compassion. He did not allow the dragon to put His fire out. By refusing to focus on Himself, and instead seeing the multitude in front of Him, compassion ruled once more and kept Him from self-pity.

Looking back on our tragedy, I (Paul) realize that I felt God's heart of compassion for our people. Whether by accident or divine providence, I was very concerned for our church members. Many of them were suffering in our loss and my heart went out to them in love and concern. I remember regularly calling on the Master Healer to do a restoration work in them. As the weeks went by, healing grace began to flow in many lives.

Allowing God to help you see the needs of others will slowly but surely start to rekindle the fire of God in you. Considering the world around you, and the hurts and trials of your brothers and sisters, will slowly but surely help you out of your dark season.

**Heavenly Father,**

I feel like the torrent of tragedy has drowned much of my passion. It has been hard to be zealous through my personal heartbreak. But I now realize that this is the plan of the devil. I ask You to shine the light of Your sunshine over my heart and life. Holy Spirit fill me afresh with Your wonderful love. Dry me out in Your precious presence.

Just as Your Son has compassion on others in His time of need, I ask You to provide me with someone that I can help even while I am grieving. Open my eyes to see the needs of those around me that I may show Your love and mercy to others.

Have Your way in my life and direct my steps.

In Jesus' name I pray,

Amen.

# Chapter 10

# GOD IS FOR YOU

During one of his darkest times, the apostle Peter received an important revelation from Christ Himself. The Bible tells us that satan had sought to sift Peter like wheat, to separate him from his friends and his destiny. But instead of Jesus praying that Peter wouldn't fail during this time of fiery trial, He prayed that Peter's *faith* wouldn't fail (see Luke 22:31-32).

This is a marvelous insight for those of us who may be interceding for loved ones in times of testing or calamity. Praying that a person's faith won't fail is as important, if not more so, than praying for the person themselves.

Even in the midst of the devastation of Ziklag, David's faith did not fail. He knew that calamity was not God's plan for his life. We must know this, too. Hannah, the mother of the one who anointed David as king, put it this way: "He raises the poor from the dust and lifts the beggar from the ash heap to set them among princes and make them inherit the throne of glory." (1 Samuel 2:8)

# The Undeniable Goodness of God

The Bible says that God's plans for us are: "Good, to give us a future and a hope." (Jeremiah 29:11). In the midst of calamity, reminding yourself of the truth that God is for you and not against you is sometimes difficult. But it is vitally important.

Well-meaning onlookers will sometimes tell you that the water of affliction which is spewed out of the dragon's mouth is holy because it is painful. Or that God Himself is the author of your pain. Pain is not holy; it's just painful. And God is the One seeking to lead you out of the mire.

Psalm 34:19 is clear: "Many are the afflictions of the righteous, but The Lord delivers them out of them all." It is God alone who can lead us out of the agony of tragedy. All too often we cut ourselves off in anger or disappointment from the only One who can really help. After our sweetheart died, my wife and I were very honest with God. We told Him that we would rather have our daughter back, but that if we couldn't have her, we would take whatever help was going. We felt in desperate need and asked Him to heal our hearts and lives. We were poor in spirit.

# Restoring Trust

If your faith has been shaken or your trust in God broken through painful experiences, I encourage you to come to God in prayer. Be honest and tell Him exactly how you feel. Afterwards, I suggest you ask Him to restore your damaged faith and your broken heart. It's in His arms of love that you can be healed.

We have made a decision to stand against griefs and sorrows, and to stand in faith until we are free from both. We suggest you do the same. This is not a process of denying pain, but facing it, giving it to God, and not letting go of His hand until He has completely healed you by His love and power.

You need to boldly declare: "Devastation is not my portion" during your darkest days. You need to know that your Heavenly Father is *for* you in your time of trial, or you may never rise again.

Traveling across a different terrain often requires a different vehicle. Similarly, different types of tragedy require different sacrifices and decisions to bring full recovery. In every situation, we need to know for sure that God is on our side. He is the Answer, He is our Healer, and He is the Way Out.

An experience can be so devastating that it may feel as if there can be no life afterwards. We read the story of a man who lost his wife, his mother, and his two daughters in a car accident. But even he had a story of recovery and healing.

And we can testify that there is abundant life after disaster. Not just a second-rate existence clouded by previous calamity, but a life of joy and gladness. As God's healing grace was poured out in Jesus, we began to regard our time of tragedy as a journey to restoration *not* a permanent relocation.

# Life After Death

I (Jo) remember how important it was for me to choose life again, and to choose to believe God for a good future. I intentionally decided to believe the Lord for His very best to come to pass. I did not allow myself to accept that my days of true happiness were over. The words of an old song became an anthem: "I have a living hope, I have a future, God has a plan for me, of this I'm sure!"

Our hero David put it this way in one of his songs: "Though I walk through the valley of the shadow of death..." (Psalm 23:4) Another psalmist wrote: "Blessed are those whose strength is in you, who have set their hearts on pilgrimage. As they pass through the valley of Baca..." (Psalm 84:5-6) The word Baca means weeping. We do not walk to the valley of the shadow of death; we walk through it. We do not remain in a wilderness of weeping; we pass through it on our way to restoration.

God has given us a way to travel safely out of tragedy's gates. David reached for a piece of equipment which God had given to the priests of Israel: the linen ephod. It was a garment worn by priests when seeking direction from God on behalf of the nation. It represented many things – the love relationship between God and His chosen people, the ministry, and the presence of the Holy Spirit, to name a few.

With the ephod, David went to the Lord: "And David enquired of the Lord saying, 'Shall I pursue this band? Shall I overtake them?' And He said to him, 'Pursue for you shall surely overtake them, and you shall surely recover all.'" (1 Samuel 30:8)

# Please Don't Give Up

The Lord says something here that I believe He is saying to all His people in similar circumstances: "It's NOT over." Specifically, He told David to pursue, overtake, and recover all. From a natural point of view, David and his men didn't even know which way the captors went. They went anyway.

Understand that God has an exit strategy for you which will carry you out of every tragedy. 2 Corinthians 2:14 puts it this way: "Thanks be to God who always causes us to triumph in Christ."

Please don't give up until you get this triumph. You will know when that is. Reach for *your* ephod (it may be worship, certain scriptures, a particular healing message) and set your heart on pursuing wholeness. You will surely come through victorious. Let's pray.

**Heavenly Father,**

Thank You, Lord, that You are with me, and You are for me, even in the midst of tragedy.

(*If you ever felt that God was against you, pray with us here*): I am sorry, Lord, that I thought You were my problem. Please forgive me. I thought You were against me. I believed You let me down. But now I know that's not true. You are not the author of my pain, You are for me, You love me, and You will lead me out.

I will not give up until I experience victory in my life. I will pursue my healing and keep my eyes fixed on You, Jesus. Thank You because You will lead me out of the valley of weeping and into restoration. You have a good future ahead for me and I give You all the praise.

In Jesus' name I pray,

Amen.

# Chapter 11

# LOVE IS STRONGER

As you may know if you have already been through a tragedy, it affects everyone differently and people react in all sorts of ways. Immediately after Naomi's death, I (Jo) went out and got some huge photographs of our daughter printed. I put them up all over the house. To Paul, they looked really weird. But they were helping me to cope. Paul gave me the space to grieve in my own way, just as he needed the space to grieve in his. On several occasions, I left the house for the best part of a day to allow Paul the solitude he needed to grieve without anyone around. On other occasions, he retreated to gardening.

There are things we know that for love's sake we should do. These things, like forgiveness, can be incredibly difficult in terrible circumstances. But no matter how hard it seems, our enemies are *never* flesh and blood, even if it looks like it one hundred per cent. God has equipped us all with three great abiding gifts from the Holy Spirit: faith, hope, and love (see 1 Corinthians 13:13). The greatest one is love.

Faith may fail. We know Jesus prayed that Peter's faith *wouldn't* fail, so there was clearly the possibility that it might have done. Hope may dwindle. Proverbs 13:13 explains that "Hope deferred makes the heart sick." However, love never fails (see 1 Corinthians 13:8).

# Love In Action

It is important to show love towards people at all times, but especially if human agency caused your pain. Someone may have run off with your money or your spouse; someone (as in our case) may have had some responsibility for the death of your loved one.

We deliberately chose to forgive the doctor who didn't diagnose that our child was very sick. The inquiry into Naomi's death exposed the fact that a simple injection of antibiotics, administered at an early stage of the illness, would probably have saved her life – at a cost of ten dollars.

Every time we prayed about our tragedy, we mentioned the doctor by name and blessed her. We asked God to make sure that this mistake did not haunt her. We also prayed that she would gain any skills which she presently lacked, so that the next time she was faced with a similar situation, her decisions would save lives. Love never fails.

# The Power of Forgiveness

We are convinced that our healed hearts today are in part the result of loving prayers and a willingness to forgive back then. Kenneth Hagin, the great preacher of love and faith, once said that refusing to forgive someone is like drinking poison in the hope that the other person will die. We have seen first-hand that walking in forgiveness is like drinking new life into your soul.

If you need to forgive someone, why don't you do it today? Be specific and tell the Lord in prayer who you are forgiving, and tell Him exactly what you are forgiving them for. You will feel a burden lift from your shoulders. Going a step further and praying for a perpetrator's wellbeing and blessing will bring healing and favor to your life. It's not always easy, but it's the right thing to do. We have clear encouragement from the Scriptures.

The Holy Spirit through the apostle Paul said in Romans 12:14: "Bless those who persecute you; bless and do not curse." Jesus, our example, put it this way: "But I tell you: love your enemies and pray for those who persecute you." (Matthew 5:44) And again in Luke 6:27-28, He said: "But I tell you who hear me: love your enemies, do good to those who hate you. Bless those who curse you, pray for those who mistreat you."

Unfortunately, some so-called Christian teachers have led whole denominations to pray for calamity to fall on their enemies and have taught their people to pray for bad things to happen to those who have wronged them. This activity, according to the Bible, is contrary to wisdom. It opens up the heart of a person to hatred, not Christian love.

# God's Perspective

When David's son Solomon ascended to the throne of Israel, God asked him to request one thing. Solomon asked for wisdom, and this was God's reply: "Because you had this in mind, and not to ask for riches, wealth or honour, or for the life of those who hate you, ... Wisdom and knowledge I grant unto thee; riches and wealth and honour such as none of the kings have had before thee." (2 Chronicles 1:11-12)

God granted his request with powerful results. Solomon ruled and reigned over the most prosperous kingdom ever, relative to the wealth on earth at that time. This was as much about what he *didn't* ask for as it was about what he *did* ask for. Allow the love of God to rise within you so that you can live in the freedom and joy of forgiveness, generosity of spirit, and mercy. It will help set you free to start enjoying life after tragedy. Let's pray.

**Heavenly Father,**

There are people who have hurt me in the middle of tragedy. Their wrongs feel even worse because of the consequences or because of the timing. But I make a choice today to forgive those who have hurt me.

I forgive _____ (insert their name) for the things they did or did not do that hurt me. (*Now tell the Lord exactly what they did that wounded you. Explain the impact and how you felt.*) But today I choose to forgive, because You always forgive me. I let go of what they did that hurt me and I let go of any debt they may owe.

I release them to You, Lord God, and I ask You to bless and help them.

Thank You for the freedom of walking in love. Help me to love others and be gracious to others in every situation.

I love You, Lord.

In Jesus' name,

Amen.

# Chapter 12

# THE WANDERING EGYPTIAN

There is an interesting phenomenon in the lives of God's people which we call 'the wandering Egyptian'. We encourage you to study the story of Ziklag in the Bible for yourself; as you do, God will use the passages to open your eyes to many great truths. 1 Samuel 30 is a template for restoration.

The Holy Spirit, through the writings of Paul, teaches us that no matter how hard the circumstances, "Love never fails." (See 1 Corinthians 13:8) The Scripture expounds: "Love is patient, love is kind..." (1 Corinthians 13:4)

It was in reading, studying, and listening to the teachings of others that I (Paul) grasped the wandering Egyptian principle. How we conduct our lives on a day-to-day basis can affect the outcome of potentially catastrophic situations. God uses the compassion that He places in our hearts to bring about circumstances that work in our favor. Even when our motives are purely to help, He will find a way to reward us.

# The Power of Kindness

In the original story, our hero David had lost everything. His entire group was devastated. Yet while they were on the road searching for their enemy, at a time when every resource and every minute counted, they stopped in their tracks to show unmerited kindness to an Egyptian who was in a similar situation to their own (see 1 Samuel 30:10-11). Abandoned by his master due to sickness, this young man was lost and dying.

One might reasonably have thought: 'What have I got to do with this man? I have enough trouble of my own. Time is running out. Water is running out. Walk on by.' But examining this story closely exposes the fact that God likes to hide the solution to a problem in the most unlikely of places. They fed him, gave him a drink, and then waited until his spirit had revived. Food and water will have been scarce in this desolate place. They shared even in their lack.

It is all too easy to be so consumed with our circumstances that we become bound by self-pity. But we can see God's purposes when we shift our focus away from our own situations. The key to activating the wandering Egyptian principle is to look outside your own situation and show kindness to others. Because we seldom know which wandering Egyptian holds the key to our blessing, we must show as much kindness to as many wandering Egyptians as circumstances permit.

This Egyptian became the solution to David's problem. He told our hero where the Amalekites (the people who had kidnapped the men's families) had gone. As a result, David and his band of warriors were able to launch a counterattack and take back what the enemy had stolen.

And the moral of the story? Be kind, even when it is painfully difficult. You never know how far your kindness will take you. Our prayer is that, like David, your kindness will take you all the way through to absolute victory – no matter what your own personal story. Let's pray.

**Heavenly Father,**

I ask for Your help to be kind to the people around me, even while I am suffering myself. Help me to walk in love and to be patient. Help me to remember the needs and issues of others in the midst of my own difficulties.

Help me to be more like Your Son.

In Jesus' name I pray,

Amen.

# Chapter 13

# ESCAPE TO VICTORY

Our battle is never against flesh and blood. But we must crave vengeance against the invisible forces which conspire against our lives to bring about calamity and devastation. In the end, King David experienced a mighty victory for his men and himself. 1 Samuel 30:17 describes the moment of triumph against their enemies: "And David slaughtered them from twilight until the evening of the next day."

Our warfare is spiritual (see Ephesians 6:10), our enemies are spiritual, and God wants us to have the victory over all our foes (see 2 Corinthians 10:4). The Bible states in 2 Corinthians 2:14 that God "...always leads us in triumph..." Being led by the Spirit (see Romans 8:14) is the same thing as being led into triumph.

If you are not yet out of the other side of your trial, please hang on and press into God in prayer for your personal breakthrough. Join one of our Heart Academy courses or one of our healing events. God will do more than you could ask or imagine. As Lamentations 2:19b says, "Pour out your heart like water before the presence of the Lord."

Know that for those who love God and who are living according to His purposes, all things – even calamities – will eventually work together for the good. We have His Word on it. (See Romans 8:28)

# Vengeance!

Isaiah 59:17 makes God's desire for vengeance against the enemy crystal clear: "Now the Lord saw, and it was displeasing in His sight that there was no justice... and He put on righteousness like a breastplate, and a helmet of salvation on His head; and He put on garments of vengeance for clothing and wrapped Himself with zeal as a mantle. According to their deeds, so He will repay. Wrath to His adversaries, recompense to His enemies."

Part of our spiritual armor is the garment of vengeance. If a bully knocked on your door to threaten you, and you chased him down the street with an axe, he would think twice about knocking on your door again. So it is with your enemy, the devil. When he knocks, let Jesus bellow at him through you. Stand your ground in faith and rise up in your authority in Christ.

1 John 3:8 says, "For this reason the Son of God was made manifest; that He may destroy the works of the devil." Jesus came to earth to annihilate satan's handiwork. We have an opportunity after we have gone through adversity to become a weapon of destruction in God's hand. Psalm 144:1 says that God wants to:

"Train our hands for warfare and our fingers for battle." Attributes like kindness and forgiveness will counteract the spirit of wickedness (see Romans 12:20-21). Love will always overpower hatred and joy will drive out depression (see Proverbs 17:22).

We were never poorer in spirit than in the days and weeks after our sweetheart died. In that time, we made a deliberate decision to seek more of God and His purposes for our lives. We resolved that what the devil had intended for our total destruction would ultimately result in a higher call in Christ's kingdom ministry.

Truly, this decision has paid off. We had every excuse and every opportunity to get offended at God, to walk away from His plan, to down tools in His vineyard. Instead, we purposed in our hearts to redouble our efforts and dedicate everything to Him afresh.

# Healing The Hurting

Possibly as a direct result of our decisions, the Lord has given us a ministry of healing and restoring broken lives worldwide. We have ministered God's healing power to countless hurting people in churches, conventions, small groups, weekends away, and even on street corners and in busy marketplaces. Now that's true vengeance.

Our recovery from tragedy did not happen overnight. It was a slow, gradual process of healing and restoration. Often, we had to revisit the painful memories and cry, weep, and mourn. Many people try to bury emotions that are too painful to face and to trap unspoken words deep inside. These trapped emotions and words can cause all sorts of complications in future life. They can cripple the soul of the strongest person. It is best to release your thoughts and feelings to God in intimate times of prayer and worship. He is able to restore. We were not created to carry such heavy weights. Jesus bore our griefs so that we would not have to.

As you receive your healing, ask God to make you a weapon of vengeance in His hand, a vessel of love and healing into the lives of others.

# Liberated to Bring Freedom

While ministering at a drug and alcohol rehabilitation center once, I (Paul) shared our experience with a group in order to help their recovery. As I told our story, a man got up from his chair and left in a hurry. Someone explained that the man's son had died in his arms twenty-four years earlier. On the night that the tragedy happened, the man had gone out seeking drugs to try and escape the pain, and he had been a heroin addict ever since.

I asked to see him after I had finished my talk. I told him that God had given me a healing ministry for people who had suffered bereavement. As I prayed for him, God's love reached deep down into his heart. Afterwards, he said to me that he felt that a huge burden had been removed from him. He started to share his story, and tears ran down his face for the first time in many, many years. From that moment on, his recovery process accelerated beyond measure.

Rehabilitation centers are often filled with people who have similarly heartbreaking stories of loss, abuse, pain, and unhealed memories. The anesthetic of drugs and alcohol can end up being the first port of call for many. This man recovered remarkably quickly, and he became a volunteer at his center, helping others who had suffered. He then went on to get a job with the responsibility of helping many people across a number of rehab houses. I saw this as a tremendous example of vengeance. If you haven't already, why don't you start to believe God for your day of vengeance?

# Unearthing Buried Pain

Tragedy doesn't necessarily have to be lengthy to be crippling. The younger and more vulnerable a person is, the more damaging a calamity can be. Many times, a young soul has been deeply wounded in the storms of life, and the depth of wounding may not be evident until odd or dysfunctional behavior manifests itself in their adult years.

Time spent in God's presence, asking Him to heal and restore, is vital. We are not suggesting a navel-gazing "Mamma didn't love me" lifestyle (sometimes lived by people who are finding an excuse for unforgiveness), but one of awareness. Victimhood never did anyone any good and can lead to crippling self-pity. We are very complex beings, and we are capable of burying deeply hurtful experiences which end up shaping our lives.

Hurt people will hurt people, but healed people can bring God's glorious healing power to others. It's much better to be well inside and out and to become a carrier of healing and well-being for others. That is true victory.

# Pursue, Overtake, and Recover All

1 Samuel 30:20 explains how David's story ended: "So David had captured all the sheep and the cattle which the people drove ahead of the other livestock, and they said, 'This is David's spoil.'" This verse is wonderful. In Ziklag, David lost everything. However, because of what he did in the midst of the ashes of a ruined life and ministry, he not only recovered everything which the enemy stole. He destroyed his enemy and ended up being more blessed than when the enemy first attacked him.

Instead of the enemy running off with his stuff, he ran off with the enemy's stuff! The same thing happened to Job. The most successful and blessed man in the ancient world, Job became the victim of a dethroned angel who was once clothed in glory and dressed in precious jewels (see Ezekiel 28:12): satan himself.

By exercising a spiritual force called patience (literally: abiding under) against his circumstances, Job eventually overcame his personal tragedy (James 5:11). The Scripture says the same about him as it did about David. Job 42:10 reads: "And the Lord restored Job's losses when he prayed for his friends, indeed the Lord gave Job twice as much as he had before."

A combination of faith, patience, and praying for others, ushered in the victory and restoration which both Job and David needed. And both lived life to the full once again after their days of devastation.

# Coming Out the Other Side

Anyone can face calamity; rich or poor, young or old, wise man or fool. It's not what we encounter, it's how we recover that matters.

James 1: 2-4 could be one of the Bible's most important verses: "Consider it all joy, my brethren, when you encounter various trials, knowing that the testing of your faith produces endurance. And let endurance have its perfect result, so that you may be perfect and complete, lacking in nothing."

What we think, say, and do whilst we're in a trial, and the kind of victory we set our sights on as we exit, are so important. After our little one died, we set our sights on having a future that would please God, a ministry that would bring Him even more glory, and a life of love.

If God brought victory for David, if God did it for Job, if God did it for us, He will do it for you. In fact, He will do it for anyone. Acts 10:34b is clear, "I most certainly understand now that God is not one to show partiality." What God will do for one, He will do for anyone who will believe.

We have prayed that the Lord will use this book as a point of contact to bring healing and restoration to your life. We would like to encourage you to reach out to God in faith right now and to receive what is yours by right, through Christ's sufferings. He was wounded for your healing. He suffered for your restoration.

# An Eternal Perspective

Paul the apostle, looking back over the difficulties of his life, gives us the following account in 2 Corinthians 11:23-27: "I have been... imprisoned, beaten numerous times, often in danger of death. Five times I received 39 lashes. Three times I was beaten with rods, once I was stoned (to death, then raised from the dead). Three times I was shipwrecked, once spending a day and a night in the deep. I have been in dangers from rivers, dangers from robbers, dangers from my countrymen, dangers from the gentiles, dangers in the city, the wilderness, the sea, dangers among false brethren; in labor and hardship, through many sleepless nights, in hunger and thirst, often without food, in cold and exposure."

The same Paul wrote in 2 Corinthians 4:17: "For momentary, light affliction is producing for us an eternal weight of glory far beyond all comparison." Because of his glimpse into the glory that awaits God's people, Paul considered his list of severe trials and troubles as "momentary light affliction". Wow! Let us have the same confession over our lives.

May the Lord turn your test into a wonderful testimony, your mess into a message of love and hope, and may the arrow sent to destroy you fail. May your life become a great demonstration of what God's power can do in anyone. We pray this for you in Jesus's name, Amen. Now, let's pray together.

**Heavenly Father,**

Thank You that You have a plan for victory. I lay my life before You now. I surrender every up and down and every twist and turn on my journey. Lord, I ask that You would take the experiences of my life and make me an instrument of healing for others. Take my pain and my mess, and turn it into a ministry that brings restoration.

May my life bring glory to You.

In Jesus' name I pray,

Amen.

# Chapter 14

# CRUCIAL LAST WORDS

Life is very beautiful. It is a rich journey whose destination is, by the grace and mercy of God, Paradise. I (Paul) remember being in my prayer chamber and thanking God for this experience we call life; my very ability to breathe, to experience joy and pain, to kiss and hug, to communicate, to see flowers, to feel rain, to be a daddy, to appreciate music. If it hasn't already, I pray that the same spirit of thanksgiving will fall on you soon – it's so wonderfully refreshing.

The misery of many people's everyday situations can easily drown out any feeling of thanksgiving. The list of griefs and sorrows we bear can be very long. The pain of loss, the stress of poverty, the bereavement and bitterness of divorce, the void of barrenness, the ghosts of the past and other such woes can kill our well-being, steal our joy, and destroy our hope. Our challenge is to rise above these afflictions into the abundant life promised by God. In John 10:10b, Jesus said: "I came that they may have life, and have it abundantly."

I (Paul) will never forget my first visit to the nation of Mozambique. It's one of the poorest countries in the world, with hardship levels that can barely be imagined. At that time, life expectancy was forty-four years for a man and forty-six for a woman. At a conference I attended, a local choir sang songs of thanksgiving. They lit up the night by singing for an hour in the cold and rain. It was very moving. Who knows what sort of home they returned to? They obviously weren't thankful for their circumstances. They were thankful *in spite of* their circumstances.

Psalm 100:4 says: "Enter His gates with thanksgiving and His courts with praise." I have concluded: "No thanksgiving? No entry." The most powerful place in existence is out of bounds to me if my heart isn't thankful. How sad. The place of eternal answers has restricted access – only the thankful get through the gates. This is worth remembering. This revelation has revolutionized my prayer life and has caused me to be a more grateful person.

# The Overflow

The application of this truth has overflowed into my life in the form of better manners, better treatment of waiting and hotel staff, and even more patience towards those whose job it is to issue parking fines (I haven't quite said "thank you" yet, but God is working on me!).

Let thanksgiving become your passport to your next blessing. Complaining, grumbling, self-pity, and general negativity will shrivel under the light of thanksgiving.

If you are from a nation, region, or family which has a propensity to whine (and you know who you are!), you will have to purpose in your heart that you will not "go the way of your fathers". Instead, you will break through into the land of thanksgiving. Thanksgiving is a powerful investment with multiple returns.

When a person's heart is heavy with the scars of griefs and sorrows, praise can be difficult. In writing this book, we have prayed that those griefs and sorrows will be totally removed from your heart and soul. We pray this book will help you on the journey to a wonderfully healed and restored future. No matter what your life's experience has been, we believe that God will make a way for His love, His peace, and His joy to multiply in your life.

**Heavenly Father,**

Thank You for Your goodness, thank You for life itself. Thank You for sustaining me even through my darkest seasons. Thank You for Your presence, for never leaving me and for always leading me out of difficulty and into victory. Thank You for Your healing love, which You have poured out for me. Thank You for Your mercies which are new every morning.

(*Now spend a few more minutes thanking the Lord.*)

I am so grateful for what You have done in my heart even as I have read this book.

I give You all the praise and all the glory.

In Jesus' name,

Amen.

# About the Authors

**Paul Naughton:** followed the call of God into full-time ministry after a successful career in banking. He has preached in major crusades, at conferences, and in churches in 27 nations across four continents. Paul has great authority in the Word and moves under a strong prophetic anointing, bringing the supernatural power of God with signs following. He has been featured on television and radio networks across Europe, Africa, and the Americas. He is Founder and Senior Pastor of Harvest Church in London, England, which he leads together with Jo. Paul is passionate about raising up mighty prayer warriors in the UK. Paul and Jo have two children, Benjy and Abby.

You can connect with Paul via www.harvestchurch. org.uk YouTube (Harvest Church London) or Instagram (@paulnaughton_)

**Jo Naughton:** is the founder of Whole Heart Ministries, which sets people free to fulfill their God-given purpose. A public relations executive turned minister, Jo's previous career included working for King Charles (while he was the Prince) as an executive VP of his largest charity. After reaching the pinnacle of the public relations world, Jo felt the call of God to full-time ministry. She is a regular guest on TV and radio shows in the US and UK.

An international speaker and author, Jo ministers with a heart-piercing anointing, sharing with great personal honesty in conferences and at churches around the world. Her passion is to see people set free from all inner hindrances so that they can fulfill their God-given destiny. Countless people have testified to having received powerful and life-changing healing through her ministry. You can join Jo's Mentoring Network, access one of her courses at The Heart Academy or attend any of her virtual or in person conferences. Visit JoNaughton.com

Connect with Jo via JoNaughton.com, Instagram (@jonaughton_), YouTube (Jo Naughton), Facebook (Jo Naughton)

www.ingramcontent.com/pod-product-compliance
Lightning Source LLC
Chambersburg PA
CBHW051847040426
42447CB00006B/740